P · O · C · K · E · T · S

ASTROLOGY

NEPTUNE

CAPRICORN IN
THE ZODIAC
WHEEL

LIBRA – THE SCALES

P · O · C · K · E · T · S

ASTROLOGY

Written by
DARBY COSTELLO
and
LINDSAY RADERMACHER

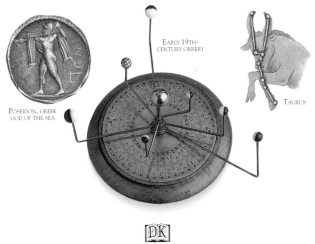

EARLY 19TH-
CENTURY ORRERY

POSEIDON, GREEK
GOD OF THE SEA

TAURUS

DK

A DK PUBLISHING BOOK

Project editor	Scarlett O'Hara
Design assistant	Andrea Jeffrey-Hall
Senior editor	Alastair Dougall
Senior art editor	Sarah Crouch
Production	Josie Alabaster
	Katie Holmes
Picture research	Sam Ruston
US editor	Constance M. Robinson

First American Edition, 1996
2 4 6 8 10 9 7 5 3 1
Published in the United States by
DK Publishing, Inc., 95 Madison Avenue,
New York, New York 10016

Library of Congress Cataloging-in-Publication Data
Costello, Darby.
   Astrology / by Darby Costello and Lindsay Radermacher. —
1st American ed.
      p.   cm. — (Pockets)
   Summary: Provides an introduction to the history and practice
of astrology.
   ISBN 0 7894 1019-2
   1. Astrology—Juvenile literature. [1. Astrology.]
I. Radermacher, Lindsay. II. Title. III. Series.
BF1708.1.C67 1996
133.5—dc20   96–15761
                                                   CIP
                                                    AC

Color reproduction by Colourscan, Singapore
Printed and bound in Italy by L.E.G.O.

CONTENTS

How to use this book

These pages show you how to use *Pockets: Astrology*. The book is divided into five sections. The sections contain information on different aspects of astrology and the signs of the zodiac. At the beginning of each section there is a picture page and a guide to the contents of that section.

HEADING
This describes the subject of the page. This page is about the zodiac sign of Leo. If a subject continues over several pages, the same heading applies.

INTRODUCTION
This provides you with a summary and overview of the subject. After reading the introduction, you should have a clear idea of what the following page, or pages, are about.

Corner coding

Heading

Introduction

Caption

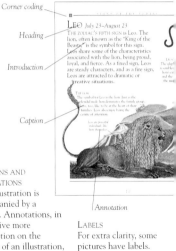

■ LEO *July 23–August 23*
THE ZODIAC'S FIFTH SIGN is Leo. The lion, often known as the "King of the Beasts" is the symbol for this sign. Leos share some of the characteristics associated with the lion, being proud, loyal, and fierce. As a fixed sign, Leos are steady characters, and as a fire sign, Leos are attracted to dramatic or creative situations.

THE LION
The symbol for Leo is the lion. Just as the lion has a pride, so too does the Leo. Leos, too, like to be at the heart of their families. Leos also enjoy being the center of attention.

Leos are proud individuals, like their namesakes.

Annotation

CORNER CODING
The corners of the main section pages are color-coded to remind you which section you are in.

■ THE PLANETS
■ SIGNS OF THE ZODIAC
■ TECHNIQUES

CAPTIONS AND ANNOTATIONS
Each illustration is accompanied by a caption. Annotations, in *italics*, give more information on the features of an illustration, and there are usually leader lines to point out details of the picture.

LABELS
For extra clarity, some pictures have labels. These identify a picture if this is not immediately obvious from the text.

RUNNING HEADS

These remind you which section you are in. The top of the left-hand page gives the section name, and the top of the right-hand page gives the subject heading.

GLYPHS

Many of the pages in this book show symbols called glyphs. The planets and signs of the zodiac are represented by glyphs. This is the glyph for Aquarius.

Running head

MOON SIGNS

THE MOON MOVES quickly through the zodiac, completing its cycle in 28 days. The Sun and Moon are a complementary pair in the birth chart, but, though everyone knows their Sun sign, few people know their Moon sign.

Label   Fact box

FACT BOXES

Many pages have fact boxes. These provide at-a-glance information about the subject, such as the ruling planet of a zodiac sign.

REFERENCE SECTION

The reference pages are yellow and appear at the back of the book. On these, you will find a chart where you can work out your Moon sign. There is also a list of useful addresses on the Resources pages.

INDEX AND GLOSSARY

At the back of the book is an index listing every subject in the book. By referring to the index, information on particular topics can be found quickly. A glossary defines the technical terms used in the book.

INTRODUCTION TO ASTROLOGY

WHAT IS ASTROLOGY?

SINCE ANCIENT TIMES, people have
seen a link between the patterns
in the heavens and the patterns
of life on Earth. Using the stars
as a guide, astrologers see the
patterns in the birth chart as
a reflection of
the life of
the individual.

OUR HOME PLANET
We know that the Earth and
other planets orbit the Sun. But
for us human beings, the Earth is
the center of the universe.

STARGAZER
Since the beginning of time,
humans have looked at the
heavens in awe. Babylonian
stargazers saw patterns in
the night sky more than
3,000 years ago.

CELESTIAL ATLAS
The Sun's apparent
progress through the
constellations, and the
Moon's phases as it circles
the Earth, have always
fascinated sky watchers.

ROYAL
FUNERAL
MASK

Most astrologers use a computer to calculate the chart

BIRTH CHART

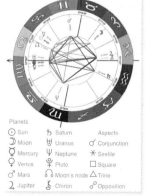

MASK OF A KING

In ancient times, birth charts or horoscopes were set up for kings and rulers. This assumed that the destiny of the ruler was central to the destiny of his people. Today, we are more interested in our own personal development.

THE MODERN BIRTH CHART

Now it is easy for anyone to have a birth chart drawn up. The chart represents the celestial patterns in the form of a diagram, which an astrologer can interpret. It is a map of the positions of the Sun, Moon, and planets seen from a particular time and place on Earth.

Planets			Aspects	
☉ Sun	♄ Saturn		♂ Conjunction	
☽ Moon	♅ Uranus		⚹ Sextile	
☿ Mercury	♆ Neptune		□ Square	
♀ Venus	♇ Pluto		△ Trine	
♂ Mars	☊ Moon's node		☍ Opposition	
♃ Jupiter	⚷ Chiron			

Common misunderstanding:

Astrology is concerned with reading the
patterns that the Sun, Moon, and
planets make against the background
of stars in the zodiac. Astrologers try to
discover what the patterns reflect
about life here on Earth. Astrology
is commonly confused with other studies,
such as palm reading, crystal-ball reading, or
reading tea leaves. But none of these is
related to astrology.

BLACK MAGIC
Sometimes astrology is confused
with black magic, and people are
afraid to look at it seriously.
Astrology has nothing to do
with witches or spells.

PALMISTRY
Palmistry reads the
lines and shapes
the hand to
foretell events
The study has
no connection
with astrolo

The lines on
the hand
form patterns

Pattern is
important in
astrology, to

READING THE LEAVES
Some people are able to see
pictures in the tea leaves at
the bottom of a cup. This
art is unrelated to astrology.

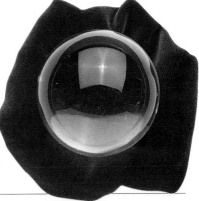

FINGER OF FATE
Many people
believe astrologers
can tell you what
will happen in
the future and
can give you
specific directions. Modern astrologers do not
pretend to see everything in your birth chart. Nor will
they tell you what to do. They try to show
the possibilities and opportunities available at any time.

FINGER OF
FATE

CRYSTAL-BALL GAZING
Some people can look into a crystal ball and see
events and people in other times and places. This
ancient practice has nothing to do with astrology.

MAGAZINE HOROSCOPES
Many magazines and newspapers
have Sun sign columns. Many
astrologers believe they are
misleading because their forecasts
are based only on the Sun signs
and not on the whole birth chart.

HISTORY OF ASTROLOGY

EARLY REFLECTING
TELESCOPE
(1671)

THE ORIGINS OF ASTROLOGY are lost in the mists of time. Mesopotamian stargazers, around 1800 BC, recorded their astronomical observations of lunar movements and eclipses. The first astrological texts were written for students 2,000 years ago, and the earliest-known horoscope dates from 409 BC.

c.5BC	AD 787	1473

- c.5BC A zodiac of 12 30° signs and early horoscopes emerge in Babylonia.

ENGRAVING OF PTOLEMAIC
UNIVERSE (1708)

- c.AD 100–178 Greek philosopher Ptolemy catalogs the stars in his book *Almagest*. In *Tetrabiblos*, astrology is given a scientific basis.

- 787–886 Persian astrologer Abu Ma'shar studies and correlates cycles of planetary relationships. His work influences European astrologers until the 16th century.
- c.1220 Guido Bonatti, Italian astrologer, writes *Liber Astronomiae*, the main textbook used by medieval astrologers.
- 1433–1499 Italian Renaissance physician, priest, philosopher, and astrologer Marsilio Ficino introduces the idea of spiritual and psychological astrology.

ENGRAVING OF COPERNICAN
UNIVERSE (1660)

- 1473–1543 Nicolaus Copernicus, a Polish astronomer educated in Italy, in his book *De Revolutionibus* (1543), does not distinguish between astronomy and astrology. He argues that the Sun, and not the Earth, is at the center of the solar system.

| 1505 | 1571 | 1875 |

EARLY HOROSCOPE (1505)

• 1505 Early horoscopes use only the Sun, Moon, and visible planets.

ELIZABETH I OF ENGLAND (1533–1603)

• 1533–1603 Queen Elizabeth I is greatly influenced by astrology. Her court astrologer, John Dee, is respected as a great scholar.

• 1564–1642 Italian astronomer Galileo Galilei develops the telescope to expand his view of the heavens.

JOHANNES KEPLER (1571–1630)

• 1571–1630 German astronomer Johannes Kepler formulates laws of planetary motion and works to demonstrate the link between them and the cycles on Earth.

• 1583–1659 Morin de Villefranche, a French mathematician and astrologer, in his book *Astronomica Gallica*, sets out to increase the accuracy of natal astrology.

• 1602–1681 English astrologer William Lilly is credited with predicting the English Civil War (1642–47), the Great Plague (1665), and the Great Fire (1666). In *Christian Astrology* he shows that astrology allows for free will.

• 1860–1917 Englishman Alan Leo brings the spiritual ideas of theosophy to astrology.

CARL JUNG (1875–1961)

• 1875–1961 The Swiss psychologist Carl Jung influences the growth of psychological astrology. His work on "archetypes" helps to form new ways of thinking about signs and planets.

• 1895–1985 American symbolic astrologer Dane Rudhyar expands on the psychological and mythical thinking of Jung.

• c.1980s Astrologers use computers for long calculations and to plot the positions of planets.

PLOTTING A CHART

Computer software produces a birth chart

ASTRONOMY

ASTRONOMY AND ASTROLOGY had
close links until the development
of scientific study in the
17th century. From then on,
astronomers considered astrology
impossible to prove. Modern
astrologers use astronomical tables
to plot the positions of the planets.

ANCIENT ORRERY
This clockwork model of
the solar system, known as
an orrery, shows the Sun
orbited by Earth, which is
in turn orbited by the
Moon. The orrery reflects
British physicist Sir Isaac
Newton's (1642– 1727)
view of the universe as a
giant machine.

ASTRONOMY FACTS

✷ The word "zodiac" is
from a Greek word that
means "life."

✷ Polish astronomer
Nicolaus Copernicus
(1473– 1543) was the
first modern astronomer
to place the Sun at the
center of the universe.

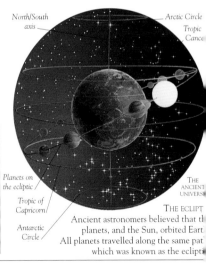

North/South axis

Arctic Circle

Tropic of Cancer

Planets on the ecliptic

Tropic of Capricorn

Antarctic Circle

THE ANCIENT UNIVERSE

THE ECLIPTIC
Ancient astronomers believed that the
planets, and the Sun, orbited Earth.
All planets travelled along the same path,
which was known as the ecliptic.

Aries

Earth

Pisces

Taurus

Celestial sphere

Celestial
equator

Aquarius

Capricorn

Gemini

Cancer

Leo

Aquarius

THE FIXED
ZODIAC
AROUND EARTH

Virgo

Sagittarius

Ecliptic

Libra

Scorpio

THE CELESTIAL SPHERE
From Earth, the stars and
planets appear to lie in an
imaginary shell around
Earth. This shell is known
as the celestial sphere.
The planets move along
the apparent path
of the Sun (the ecliptic)
against a background of
the twelve groups of stars
known as the zodiac.

CONSTELLATIONS
Early stargazers linked
groups of stars together
in patterns called
"constellations." The
twelve zodiac constellations
have been given names that
describe their shape in the sky.

19

CONSTELLATIONS

SEEN FROM EARTH, the stars appear to form patterns in the sky. The patterns are known as constellations. There are twelve constellations that correspond to the twelve signs of the zodiac. These constellations form a backdrop of stars against which the Sun, Moon, and planets appear to move during the course of a year. The Sun takes about a month to travel through each of the zodiac signs.

ARIES
MARCH 21 – APRIL 20

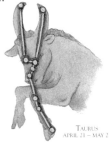

TAURUS
APRIL 21 – MAY 21

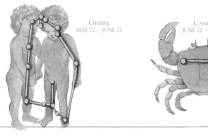

GEMINI
MAY 22 – JUNE 21

CANCER
JUNE 22 – JULY 22

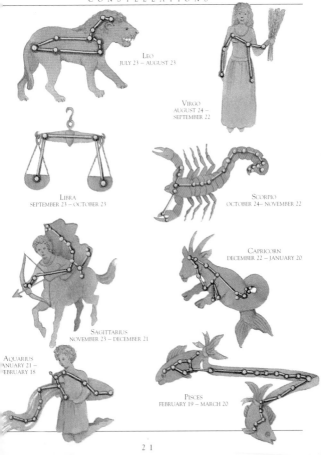

LEO
JULY 23 – AUGUST 23

VIRGO
AUGUST 24 –
SEPTEMBER 22

LIBRA
SEPTEMBER 23 – OCTOBER 23

SCORPIO
OCTOBER 24– NOVEMBER 22

CAPRICORN
DECEMBER 22 – JANUARY 20

SAGITTARIUS
NOVEMBER 23 – DECEMBER 21

AQUARIUS
JANUARY 21 –
FEBRUARY 18

PISCES
FEBRUARY 19 – MARCH 20

The northern skies

At night, when no landmarks were visible, early travelers in the desert or at sea used the stars to navigate their journeys. Star maps show the stars visible in either the Northern or the Southern Hemisphere.

THE STAR MAP
In the Northern Hemisphere the northern half of the celestial sphere can be seen. The latitude of the observer, the time of the year, and the time of night determine which stars are visible to an observer.

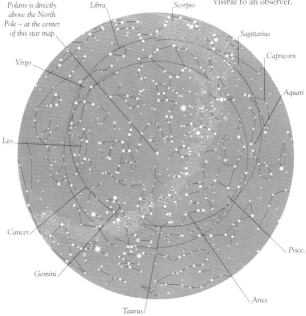

Polaris is directly above the North Pole – at the center of this star map

Libra

Scorpio

Sagittarius

Capricorn

Aquarii

Virgo

Leo

Cancer

Gemini

Taurus

Aries

Pisce

The southern skies

Ancient voyagers created pictures from the millions of stars overhead at night, to use as a guide for their journeys. Stars in both hemispheres were grouped together and given names according to their outlines.

The southern half of the celestial sphere consists of constellations visible in the Southern Hemisphere. The stars rotate around the center of the star map, a point directly above the Earth's South Pole.

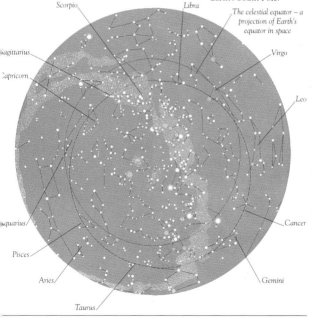

Scorpio

Libra

The celestial equator – a projection of Earth's equator in space

Sagittarius

Virgo

Capricorn

Leo

Aquarius

Cancer

Pisces

Aries

Gemini

Taurus

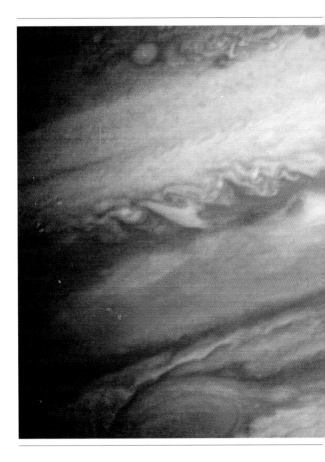

THE PLANETS

ASTROLOGICAL PLANETS

IN ASTROLOGY, the Sun, the Moon, and the eight planets – Mercury, Venus, Mars, Jupiter, Saturn, Uranus, Neptune, and Pluto – symbolize energies and patterns of behavior that are common to everyone. Astrology is a symbolic language. It is concerned with interpreting the movements of the planets and explaining how they mirror life here on Earth.

STUDYING THE STARS
Before telescopes were invented, early stargazers viewed the planets with the naked eye. They thought of the planets as gods, moving across the sky in predictable cycles.

PLANET FACTS

★ The word "planet" comes from the Greek word for "wanderer" – the planets appeared to wander the night sky.

★ There are nine planets in our solar system, including Earth.

CARL JUNG
Swiss psychologist Carl Jung (1875-1961) developed a theory that related "archetypes," or particular psychological types, to certain planets.

19TH-CENTURY ORRERY
This orrery shows seven planets circling the Sun. Neptune and Pluto are not shown; they were not found until later (1846 and 1930, respectively). The orbits are shown as circular although they are, in fact, elliptical.

Jupiter

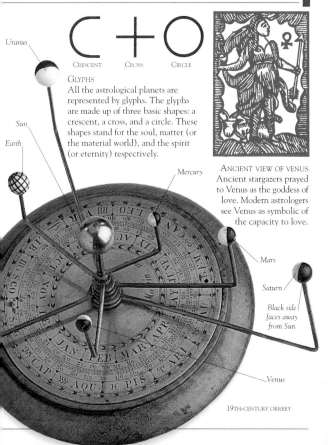

C + O

CRESCENT   CROSS   CIRCLE

GLYPHS
All the astrological planets are
represented by glyphs. The glyphs
are made up of three basic shapes: a
crescent, a cross, and a circle. These
shapes stand for the soul, matter (or
the material world), and the spirit
(or eternity) respectively.

ANCIENT VIEW OF VENUS
Ancient stargazers prayed
to Venus as the goddess of
love. Modern astrologers
see Venus as symbolic of
the capacity to love.

Uranus

Sun

Earth

Mercury

Mars

Saturn

*Black side
faces away
from Sun*

Venus

19TH-CENTURY ORRERY

THE SUN

AS THE SUN (technically
a star and not a planet)
is the source of energy
at the center of our solar
system, so in astrology it
stands for the vital,
creative force at the
center of each one of us.
In the birth chart the
Sun indicates how we
express ourselves
most naturally.

LOUIS XIV KING
OF FRANCE
(1638–1715) WAS
KNOWN AS THE
SUN KING

SUNFLOWER
As the Sun travels across the sky, the sunflower
turns toward it. This symbolizes our instinct to
look to the Sun as the source of life and vitality.

SUN KING
The Sun stands for
kings or rulers. It
has associations
with heroism and
with pride. It is
often considered a
"masculine" symbol
and linked to
strength and
courage – traditional
male attributes.

AFRICAN GOLD BRACELET

GOLD BRACELET
Gold is often linked with the Sun. Since ancient times gold has been regarded as a precious metal. The Sun as Earth's source of light and heat is also very precious.

ATHER AND CHILD
he Sun represents an essentially masculine form creative energy and is associated with fathers d people in authority. In a birth chart, the acement of the Sun indicates the guiding force someone's life. The position of the Sun at rth reveals the field in which their creativity ight flourish.

SUN FACT BOX

✳ The Sun's day is Sunday.

✳ Its body part is the heart.

✳ Its metal is gold.

✳ The Sun rules Leo and the Fifth house.

SUN GLYPH
The circle representing the spirit, or eternity, has a dot at its center. The dot suggests the emergence of life out of chaos.

THE SUN
The Sun is the center of our solar system and the star around which Earth and the other planets orbit. It is Earth's source of light and heat.

THE MOON

IN ASTROLOGY, the Moon is opposite yet
complementary to the Sun. In contrast to the Sun's
masculine attributes, the Moon is associated with
feminine, nurturing qualities. In the birth chart the
Moon represents childhood and our habit patterns.
It also stands for our instinctive responses to people
or situations, and our relationship with our bodies.

*The Moon takes
27.3 days to
orbit Earth*

MOON'S CYCLE

The Moon moves through the twelve
zodiac signs in less than a month. As it
moves around the Sun it reflects the
Sun's light and appears, from Earth, to
grow bigger (wax), become full, grow
smaller (wane), and disappear from sight.

THE SEAS AND TIDES

From early times, the Moon has been
associated with the tides. As the Moon
orbits Earth, its gravity pulls the seas
and oceans and creates the twice-daily
tides. It is astrologically connected with
the rhythms of emotional life.

MOTHER AND CHILD
In astrology, the Moon is regarded as a feminine planet. It is traditionally a symbol for mothers and mothering as well as for infancy and childhood. In a birth chart, the Moon represents connections with the past.

The Moon's gravitational pull causes the tides

MOON FACT BOX

✳ The Moon's day is Monday.

✳ Its body parts are the stomach, breasts, and womb.

✳ Its metal is silver.

✳ The Moon rules Cancer and the Fourth house.

MOON GLYPH
The glyph of the Moon is the crescent that represents the soul. It resembles the appearance of a new Moon.

THE MOON
The Moon is Earth's only satellite. It is a quarter of the size of Earth. It has been the focus of myths since early times.

MERCURY

MERCURY HAS the swiftest orbit of all the planets. To astrologers, Mercury represents the idea of communication. Mercury's attributes can be likened to those of the brain – processing and sending out information. Mercury is linked with receiving and giving out information and with mental activity.

Modern cycle courier delivers messages like mythological Mercury

MARKET

Mercury is associated with buying and selling. In a birth chart, Mercury would indicate trading, exchange, or less honest activities such as theft. It is also linked with cunning and sharp wits.

MESSENGER

Mercury is known as the messenger of the Gods. He was swift-moving, like human thought processes. In the birth chart, Mercury is related to making connections with people and places.

STUDYING
People with Mercury prominent in their birth chart will have an inquiring mind. They are keen students, endlessly investigating the world by reading, talking, and observing their fellow beings.

TELEPHONE
Mercury represents the urge to understand and to communicate. It indicates an urge to keep in touch with others, whether by phone, fax, or letter. The position of Mercury in a birth chart shows the way someone thinks and expresses themselves.

Hermes is god of winged thoughts

HERMES STATUE
In Greek mythology Mercury is known as Hermes. He is the wing-footed messenger of the Gods. He is able to move from the heights of Olympus (home of the Gods) to the depths of Hades with ease.

MERCURY FACT BOX
✳ Mercury's day is Wednesday. There is a link between Mercury and the Norse god Woden (or Odin). From Woden comes our word Wednesday.

✳ It rules Gemini and the Third house and Virgo and the Sixth house.

MERCURY GLYPH
The crescent of the soul sits above the circle of spirit and the cross of matter.

THE PLANET MERCURY
Mercury, the planet nearest to the Sun, makes the fastest orbit. Mercury is visible from Earth only before dawn and after sunset.

VENUS

VENUS IS TRADITIONALLY linked with love and beauty. To the astrologer, Venus represents the ideal of beauty attraction, and cooperation. In a birth chart, the position of Venus indicates what someone values in life and shows how he or she expresses love. Astrologically, Venus is the counterpart of Mars

ADORNMENTS
All kinds of adornments are associated with Venu from clothes and jewelery to cosmetic The position of Venu can point to a love of luxury and also to vanity.

BEAUTY AND VALUE
Venus in a birth chart symbolizes the love of beauty and grace. It shows what we value in ourselves and in others.

PEACE AND HARMONY
People with Venus prominent in their birth charts are naturally diplomatic. Like doves, they are associated with peace-making and harmony.

GODDESS OF LOVE

The Roman goddess Venus is the goddess of love
and beauty. This famous painting by Botticelli
called the *Birth of
Venus* shows Venus
as the ideal of
beauty. In Greek
mythology, Venus
was called
Aphrodite and
was the lover
of Ares (the
Greek name
for Mars).

*According to
mythology,
Venus was
born in the sea*

*Venus was
carried ashore
in a giant
conch shell*

VENUS FACT BOX

✹ Venus's day is Friday – from
the Norse goddess Freya who
has been linked with Venus.

✹ Venus rules Taurus and the
Second house; Libra and the
Seventh house.

VENUS GLYPH
The circle representing the
spirit is above the cross of
matter (the reverse of
Mars). It resembles a mirror.

THE PLANET VENUS
Venus can be clearly seen
as a beautiful morning or
evening star. It has
traditionally had romantic
associations.

MARS

Mars is traditionally warlike and fierce

THE PLANET MARS is the blood-red planet in our solar system. In mythology, Mars is the god of war. In astrology, Mars represents direct energy. It indicates the ability to assert oneself and the instinct to survive. In a birth chart, Mars shows how we get what we want from life. In contrast to its counterpart Venus, Mars puts its own desires before those of others.

MARS MYTHOLOGY
Roman Mars was called Ares in Greek mythology. He was the warrior god of war and the lover of Venus (or Aphrodite).

EMERGENCY SERVICE
The fiery quality of Mars suggests someone who charges headlong into things. Yet Mars also has a heroic aspect; it suggests someone, like a firefighter, who rushes to save and protect others.

Mars is linked to war and destruction

COMPETITIVE SPORTS

Mars suggests vitality and energy. This can be channeled very successfully into competitive sports and other physical activities. Without an outlet, Mars's energy may turn into selfishness and aggression.

SWORD

People with Mars prominent in their birth chart can be brave but foolhardy. Their courage in ting quickly and cutting through any opposition, like a sword, may have destructive consequences.

MARS FACT BOX

✷ Mars's day is Tuesday. This comes from the French word for Tuesday, *Mardi*.

✷ It rules Aries and the First house; it corules Scorpio and the Eighth house.

MARS GLYPH

The circle of spirit with an arrow above. An earlier version had a cross instead – the opposite of Venus.

THE PLANET MARS

Mars is often called the "red planet." Its reddish color is caused by iron oxide. Red is linked with anger, as in the phrase "seeing red," meaning "getting angry."

JUPITER

IN OUR SOLAR SYSTEM, Jupiter is the largest planet. In astrology, Jupiter represents the idea of expansion (as its counterpart, Saturn, represents the idea of contraction). In a birth chart, Jupiter stands for a capacity for adventure and exploration and also suggests the growth of knowledge into wisdom. It shows the areas of our life where we are confident and where we seek fulfilment.

HORSESHOE

FOUR-LEAF CLOVER

LU
Jupiter is seen as genero
optimistic, and jovi
It stands for luck but a
for taking chances. Jupi
symbolizes faith in l
and an openne
to opportuniti
It represents confidence
opposed to cautio

SPORTS
Individuals with a strong
Jupiter in their birth cha
are drawn to sports,
especially sports involvin
risk, such as horseback
riding. They are expansiv
people who need lots of
space around them.

SEEKING ADVENTURE

People with Jupiter prominent in their birth chart are great adventurers and philosophers. They are constantly searching for new experiences. This may be through a love of traveling or by exploring new subjects and ideas. Their search is not just to gather facts, but to find meaning in life.

ZEUS

In Greek mythology, the Roman god Jupiter is called Zeus. The three Olympian brothers – Zeus, Poseidon, and Hades – shared the world between them. Zeus was the supreme sky god. He married his sister Hera and fathered many other divine beings.

JUPITER FACT BOX

✴ Jupiter's day is Thursday. Jupiter is linked to the Norse god Thor. From Thor comes the word Thursday.

✴ It rules Sagittarius and the Ninth house; it corules Pisces and the Twelfth house.

JUPITER GLYPH

In Jupiter's glyph the crescent that represents the soul is above the cross that represents matter.

THE PLANET JUPITER

Jupiter, the largest planet in our solar system, has a bright orange, banded appearance. It is beset by great storms, one of which, the Great Red Spot, is visible on its surface.

SATURN

IN ANCIENT TIMES, Saturn was thought to
be the outermost planet. Consequently, in
astrology it represents the idea of limits and
order. It is associated with the skeleton,
which gives the body form, and the skin –
the body's boundary against the world. In
the birth chart, Saturn
is linked with
self-discipline
and duty.

*The Greek Titan Cronos
came to personify
Time – this ring
suggests eternity*

*Scythe
represents
death*

HOURGLASS
Saturn is linked with
time. It carries the idea
that time is limited and
like sand in an hourglass
time is running out.
Saturn is said to limit
projects, whereas Jupiter
is said to expand them.

SATURN MYTH
In Greek mythology
Saturn is associated
with the Titan, Cronos.
According to legend
Cronos ate his children
in order to prevent
prophecy from
coming true.
The prophecy had
stated that Cronos
would be killed
by his son, Zeus.

JUDGE

Saturn's influence on individuals is like that of a wise teacher or judge. It represents the need for order and security and carries a sense of duty and responsibility.

CASTLE DEFENSES

Like a castle with a strong wall around it, Saturn in a birth chart can suggest defensiveness and caution. Saturn is associated with accepting limits, planning for eventualities, and learning from difficulties.

SATURN GLYPH

The cross representing matter sits above the crescent of the soul. It is the reverse of Jupiter's glyph.

THE PLANET SATURN

Saturn was the farthest planet known until Uranus was discovered in 1781. Its rings are a very distinctive feature. It has 18 moons, the largest of which, Titan, is as big as Mercury.

URANUS

URANUS WAS NOT discovered until 1781. The planet was revealed after the invention of the telescope. As well as advances in technology at the time of its discovery, great social change was taking place. America sought independence from Britain and a revolution occurred in France. Thus, for astrologers, Uranus symbolizes modern technology and dramatic change.

LUNAR MODULE
Technological inventions, such as those that led to space travel in the 1960s, are associated with Uranus. Uranus concerned with ideas that open up new possibilities.

MODERN OFFICE ENVIRONMENT
Uranus is connected with modern technology, such as computers, linking human beings across the planet. Astrologically, Uranus means new ideas and attitudes, change and innovation. Uranus is forward-looking and progressive.

ALBERT EINSTEIN
German-American
physicist Albert
Einstein personifies
the inventiveness
and genius of
Uranus.

LIGHTNING
Lightning flashes of intuition characterize those with
Uranus prominent. Uranus (Ouranus) was an ancient
Greek personification of the stormy heavens.

URANUS FACT BOX

✶ Uranus was first observed
by telescope in 1781 by
British astronomer
William Herschel.

✶ Uranus rules Aquarius
and the Eleventh house.

URANUS GLYPH
The cross of matter above
the circle of spirit resembles
a television aerial. It links
Uranus to technology.

THE PLANET URANUS
Uranus has an unusual orbit.
It is the only known planet
to travel around the Sun on
its side. Its angle of rotation
is tilted at 98° to the vertical.

NEPTUNE

THE PLANET NEPTUNE was discovered in 1846. Around this time ether was first used in medical operations, and there was an awakening of interest in spiritual experiences or those beyond the range of normal consciousness. Neptune symbolizes a desire to experience something out of the ordinary. The worlds of fantasy, imagination, and dreams are associated with this planet.

BUDDHA
Neptune is associated with the spiritual world. It represents meditation, prayer, or fantasy as a way to get in touch with something "otherworldly."

THE OCEANS AND SEAS
Traditionally, Neptune is linked with the sea. In astrology, Neptune is full of dark, unfathomable depths, like the seas and oceans. Individuals with Neptune prominent in their charts may feel isolated and yearn to be absorbed into the greater ocean of life

trident, a traditional ol of Greek ishermen

Poseidon was the brother of Zeus and Hades

POSEIDON
The Roman god Neptune was connected to the Greek god Poseidon. Poseidon was called "Lord of he hidden and boundless sea." His domain was a ysterious and beautiful one, full of hidden dangers.

PHOTOGRAPHY
Photography was developed around the time that Neptune was discovered. Neptune in a birth chart may indicate a desire to express ideas through music or photography.

NEPTUNE GLYPH
The glyph shows the crescent of soul over the cross of matter. Its shape resembles Neptune's trident.

THE PLANET NEPTUNE
Neptune is traditionally associated with the sea. The planet Neptune is a deep blue color caused by methane in its atmosphere. Its cloud-filled skies add to Neptune's sense of mystery.

PLUTO

PLUTO, DISCOVERED IN 1930, is associated with the splitting of the atom. For astrologers, it represents the dark, unseen forces of life and is often linked with matters beyond our control, such as war and death. At the same time, Pluto also represents the renewal that arises out of destruction.

Hades had a three-headed dog called Cerberus

Hades ruled the Underworld, the realm of the "shades" or the dead

RENEWAL AND CHANGE
Pluto is linked with the mysterious forces of life and death. Like the snake shedding its skin and renewing itself, Pluto represents the powers of renewal and change.

HADES
The Roman god Pluto was called Hades by the Greeks. Hades ruled the Underworld where, according to myth, all living things eventually had to pass. This meant that room would be left on Earth for new growth and new generations.

ANGEROUS KNOWLEDGE

dividuals with Pluto prominent in their chart are
terested in the hidden side of nature. These
dividuals can feel empowered by possessing such
cret knowledge. An example might be scientists
volved in the development of the atomic bomb.

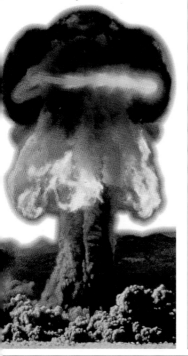

PLUTO FACT BOX

✳ Pluto was sought for many
years. It was discovered in
1930 by Clyde Tombaugh,
an American astronomer.

✳ Pluto corules Scorpio and
the Eighth house.

PLUTO GLYPH
The glyph has the cross of
matter, crescent of soul, and
circle of spirit. Sometimes
an alternative glyph is used.

THE PLANET PLUTO
As the furthest planet
in our solar system, little
information has been
gathered about Pluto. Its
remoteness adds to the
mystery that surrounds it.

CHIRON AND ASTEROIDS

ASTEROID

As well as the planets, other chunks of rock, known as asteroids, orbit the Sun. Chiron is larger than an asteroid and has been called a "centaur" by scientists. It is linked by astrologers to the mythological centaur and is associated with healers and teachers. Chiron's role in the birth chart is still being studied.

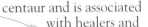

Earth

ASTEROID BELT
There is a belt of asteroids between the planets Mars and Jupiter. Some of these asteroids have been given names and are believed to have some significance in the birth chart. Chiron's orbit moves between Jupiter and Saturn and Saturn and Uranus.

CENTAUR
The centaurs were mythical creatures who were half-man and half-horse. They were wild beasts who were seen as a threat to the well-ordered world of humans. Some were wise teachers; others irresponsible revellers.

HEALER
Chiron
signifies those
who have become
healers because they
have experienced
pain themselves.

CHIRON FACTS

✷ Chiron was
discovered in 1977
by US astronomer
Charles T. Kowall.

✷ Some astrologers
believe Chiron
corules Sagittarius
with Jupiter. Others
link it with Virgo.

GLYPH
OF
CHIRON

GODDESSES AND GLYPHS OF ASTEROIDS

*Pallas Athena
is shown with
a helmet*

CERES
Ceres was the Roman
goddess of grain,
growth, and harvests.
The Greek counterpart
of Ceres is Demeter.

PALLAS ATHENA
Goddess of wisdom and
reason, Pallas Athena
(Roman goddess
Minerva) protected
heroes in battle.

VESTA
Vesta (Greek goddess
Hestia) was Roman
goddess of the hearth,
centre of the home, and
keeper of the flame.

JUNO
Juno was the goddess
of marriage. Her
Greek counterpart
was Hera, the wife or
consort of Zeus.

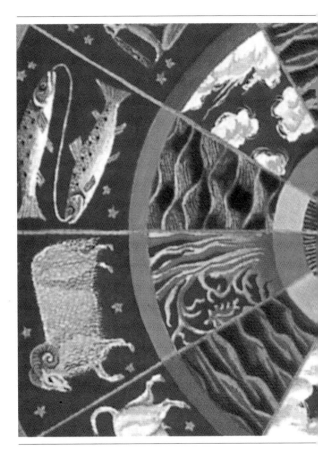

SIGNS OF THE ZODIAC

SIGN GLYPHS
AND DATES

ARIES
Mar 21–April 20

TAURUS
April 21–May 21

GEMINI
May 22–June 21

CANCER
June 22–July 22

LEO
July 23–Aug 23

VIRGO
Aug 24–Sept 22

INTRODUCTION

THE 12 SIGNS of the zodiac are denoted by
their own ancient symbols and glyphs.
Every sign is associated with certain human
characteristics and has traditional links with
particular parts of the body.

*There are
four elements*

*The 12 signs
are divided into
three qualities*

ZODIAC
WHEEL
The 12
signs are divided
into the four ancient
elements of fire, earth, air,
and water, and three qualities
cardinal (active), fixed (maintaining),
and mutable (flexible). The qualities
combine with the elements into 12
unique "types" – for example, Aries is
cardinal fire. The signs are further
split into the complementary qualities
of masculine and feminine

FIRE

EARTH   CARDINAL

AIR   FIXED   FEMININE

WATER   MUTABLE   MASCULINE

TROLOGY AND THE BODY
ce ancient times, each of the
signs has been linked
h a part of the body.
e first sign, Aries, is
ociated with the
d, and the last
n, Pisces, is
ked with the
. The other
s link up to
ans and parts
he body in
ween. In earlier
es, astrology was
ked with
dicine, especially
h the "humors,"
ch have similarities
h the four elements:
, earth, air, and water.

SIGN GLYPHS
AND DATES

LIBRA
Sept 23-Oct 23

SCORPIO
Oct 24-Nov 22

SAGITTARIUS
Nov 23-Dec 21

CAPRICORN
Dec 22-Jan 20

AQUARIUS
Jan 21-Feb 18

PISCES
Feb 19-Mar 20

ASSOCIATIONS

The following pages explore some of
the characteristics of the signs. Using
images as starting points, the interests
and motivations of the signs are
examined. For example, Sagittarians
look for patterns to try to make sense
of their existence. This image of tile
work introduces the idea of pattern.

GLYPHS

The 12 signs are represented by forms
called glyphs. Some of these are easily
recognized – for example, Aries looks
like a ram's horns. Other glyphs have
more obscure links.

ARIES *March 21–April 20*

THE FIRST SIGN of the zodiac is Aries. Accordingly, it is linked with beginnings. People born under this sign are typically enthusiastic about new events and are adventurous. The ram is the symbol for Aries and, like a ram, people with Aries prominent in their chart charge headlong into matters. Aries is a fire sign, meaning that Aries people can be exciting to know. Aries is also a cardinal (or active) sign.

ARIES GLYPH
Aries is represent
by a glyph that
suggests the hor
of a ram.

THE RAM
The symbol for Aries is the ram, an animal that has a reputation for independence. The ram is also known for using its horns to defend its territory. The ram appears in Egyptian mythology, where it represents fertility and creative force.

ZODIAC HOUSES
Aries is linked to the First house of the birth chart. This is the house of personality and indicates how someone appears at first glance.

CARDINAL

FIRE

MASCULINE

ZODIAC WHEEL

BODY PARTS
Traditionally, Aries is linked to the head. Aries people are sometimes called "headstrong" because they have a strong will.

COLOR
Red is the color associated with Aries. Red is a bold, dynamic color linked with anger.

> **RULERSHIP BOX**
>
> ✳ Aries is ruled by the planet Mars. The glyph for Mars is often used to represent male.
>
>

Aries

Aries is a sign that stands for excitement and enthusiasm for new projects. People whose birth charts show the Sun or other planets in Aries are inspired by new beginnings, new events, or new possibilities. They are also said to be willful and impulsive. They are especially good at initiating projects. They are natural pioneers.

ARIES
MARCH 21 – APRIL 20

Aries individuals will charge into the fray

Aries people have a direct and dynamic approach

BRAVE WARRIORS

Aries is associated with warriors and soldiers of all ages. Planets in Aries have a martial quality about them. Wherever Aries appears in the birth chart is an indication of where someone is brave, impetuous, or easily angered.

SHARP-EDGED

Sharp weapons such as swords are often linked with Aries. Aries people are noted for their sharp minds and sharp tongues. The energy of an Aries individual can cut through problems in a constructive or a destructive way.

Aries people can be spiky

Thistles are common in England – an Aries country

Warlike Mars rules Aries

Like this sword's blade, Aries people can be sharp

RACING AHEAD

Aries people often like fast cars that will accelerate quickly and go faster than other cars on the road. There may be a reckless and impatient streak where Aries dominates the birth chart. Aries likes to be out in front and is frustrated by slow movers.

SPIKY THISTLE

Thorny plants such as the thistle are linked with Aries. The thorns suggest Aries's direct and pointed manner. Other Aries plants include holly and hawthorn.

Aries may enjoy dangerous sports like motor racing

TAURUS *April 21–May 21*

TAURUS IS THE SECOND SIGN of the zodiac. Its symbol is a bull and the sign is known for its strength and power. It is associated with the power of nature, sometimes quiet and restful and sometimes wild and uncontrollable. Taurus is an earth sign, which means that Taureans are practical. Taurus is also called a fixed (or stable) sign.

TAURUS GLYPH
The glyph for Taurus represents the bull's head with its wide horns.

Horns have a distinctive shape

THE BULL
The symbol for Taurus is the bull. The bull is an animal that is quiet and good-natured until it is angered, when it becomes very fierce. Bulls are known to be stubborn creatures who can also be territorial. Taureans can be obstinate and possessive, too.

ZODIAC HOUSES
The Second house is linked to
Taurus. It is the house of
possessions and describes
how we feel about the
things we value.

FIXED

EARTH

FEMININE

ZODIAC WHEEL

BODY PART
Taurus is associated with the
throat and neck. Taureans
often have lovely singing and
speaking voices.

COLOR
A rich shade of pink is
linked to Taurus. Pink
flowers such as dog roses
and foxgloves are Taurean.

RULERSHIP BOX

✱ The ruler of Taurus
is Venus. The glyph for
Venus is a symbol often
used to denote female.

♀

Taurus

TAURUS
APRIL 21 – MAY 21

Taurus is a sign that has its feet firmly planted on the ground. People with the Sun or other planets in Taurus are often very patient and reliable. They do not like to be hurried and may be thought of as obstinate. Taureans have a strong appreciation of beauty and enjoy collecting beautiful objects. They are creative individuals who work methodically.

CREATING SOMETHING BEAUTIFUL
Taureans like to produce results. They are slow, careful workers who enjoy the process as much as the finished product. Taureans are most creative when the results are tangible. They like to produce things that are useful and beautiful.

WALKING IN THE COUNTRY
A love of walking in the countryside is shared by most Taureans. It is a way to calm their thoughts and find peace of mind.

USING THE VOICE
The sign of Taurus is linked with the voice. Those with Taurus prominent in their birth chart love music and singing.

Taureans are good at looking after money

MONEY AND SECURITY

Taureans function best in a secure and stable environment. Material security is very important. They prefer to spend their money on things that are practical or beautiful and valuable. Taureans feel most secure when surrounded by their possessions.

A dislike of risk or gambling is typically Taurean

LOVE OF NATURE

As an Earth sign, Taurus likes to keep in touch with nature. Taureans are not afraid to get their hands dirty to make things grow in the soil – they are often said to have "green thumbs."

GEMINI *May 22–June 21*

THE THIRD SIGN of the zodiac is Gemini. It is symbolized by the twins, indicating its dual nature. Gemini is a mutable (or changeable) sign, and Gemini people are versatile. It is also an air sign, meaning that Geminis are communicative people.

GEMINI GLYPH
Gemini is represented by a glyph made up of two lines. It indicates the two sides of the Gemini nature.

THE TWINS
Gemini's symbol is the twins. This suggests the duality of the Gemini character. Geminis may play several different roles in their lives. They are versatile and enjoy doing more than one thing at a time.

ZODIAC HOUSES
In the birth chart, the Third
House is associated with
Gemini. This house is
concerned with brothers
and sisters and
with communication.

MUTABLE

AIR

MASCULINE

ZODIAC WHEEL

BODY PART
Gemini rules the
hands, arms, shoulders, and
lungs. Geminis are quick
with their hands and
tongues, and they need
room to breathe.

COLOR
Bright colors,
especially yellow, are
typically associated
with Gemini.

RULERSHIP BOX

✴ Gemini is ruled by
the planet Mercury.
This is the glyph that
represents Mercury.

☿

GEMINI
MAY 22 – JUNE 21

Gemini

The sign of Gemini has a dualistic nature. It is a sign that is always ready to see the other point of view. Those with Gemini prominent in their birth chart are never bored with life. They are adaptable and curious characters who like to keep on the move. They are youthful and lively but can feel restless.

Geminis have a light touch

A LIGHT TOUCH

Geminis move swiftly from one project to another. They are often seen as changeable, as they move from subject to subject. However, like butterflies, they are colorful characters and can make the world a brighter place for those around them.

Geminis have a childlike fascination with the world

Geminis can flit, butterflylike, from one group of people to another

YOUTHFUL ENTHUSIASM

People with Gemini in their birth charts are interested in the world around them. Geminis are young at heart, and they never lose their desire to find out more about everything.

Geminis hide their
sadness behind a
cheerful face

JUGGLING

Life is sometimes like a
juggling act for Gemini
people. Quick-thinking and
quick-acting Geminis have no
trouble keeping several projects
going at once. They may be playful
individuals who are good mimics and
enjoy playing different roles.

Light-hearted
Geminis can be
very entertaining

The Indian Sachems cannot repass the great water
these Ample & flourishing kingdoms without expres
Just resentment & admiration for the Signal favour
from the Nobles especially of the Great Queen's Cour
Council. The Continuance of which they will endeavour
deserve by a just observance of what is expected from
renewing their belts of Wampum & what shall be put their
explained by Abadagarous Colo Nicholson as the
Pleasure of our Great Queen.

Her desire is that our Brother Quedar may see
this as our mind.

KEEPING IN TOUCH

Someone with planets in Gemini in
the birth chart likes to keep in touch.
Geminis enjoy letter-writing and tend
to be the first to know the news.

CANCER *June 22–July 22*

CANCER IS THE FOURTH SIGN of the zodiac. It is represented by a crab. The symbol of the crab suggests that people born under this sign will retreat into their shell if they feel hurt. Cancer is a cardinal sign linked with action. It is also a water sign linked with feelings.

CANCER GLYPH
The glyph for Cancer resembles two crab claws. It also suggests the rounded shape of a crab's shell.

THE CRAB
The crab is the symbol for Cancer. The crab is a hard-shelled animal with a soft body inside its shell. Like a crab, Cancer people may hide in their shell or put up barriers against outsiders. Home is very important for Cancerians.

The crab's claws are ready to grasp and hold onto its prey

Crabs move sideways; Cancerians likewise may not tackle problems head on

DIAC HOUSES
e Fourth house of the birth
art is linked with Cancer.
is house is concerned
th origins, roots,
d childhood.

ARDINAL

WATER

EMININE

ZODIAC WHEEL

BODY PART

The breasts, the womb, and the
stomach are traditionally
associated with Cancer.
Children are often very important
to those born under this sign.

COLOR

Silver gray, the color of
the sea during a storm, is
one of the colors
associated with Cancer.

RULERSHIP BOX

★ The sign of Cancer
is ruled by the Moon,
represented by the
glyph below.

Cancer

This is a sign with great sensitivity. People with the Sun or other planets in Cancer are often very kind and thoughtful. They are always aware of the needs of others. Home life is important for Cancerians; it is a place where they enjoy spending their time and where they can retreat if they feel hurt. Cancerians can be sensitive and moody.

CANCER
JUNE 22 – JULY 22

Feeding others is a source of satisfaction for Cancerians

IN THE KITCHEN
Food and cooking are very important to Cancerians. They feel contented in the kitchen, where they can feed family and friends.

SEA LOVERS
Cancer loves the sea and its treasures. Like the oyster, Cancerians have a hard protective shell.

CARING AND MOTHERING

Cancer is ruled by the Moon, which is linked with motherhood. Both male and female Cancerians are well suited to caring for others. They have an instinct to care for those who are helpless and dependent. Cancerian mothers are very protective.

Many Cancerians have a vivid recollection of their own childhoods

Cancerians need a place of retreat

HOME LIFE

Home is significant to Cancerians of all ages, whether it is a country cottage or a city apartment. A person with a strong emphasis on this sign will appreciate the protection that a home affords. It is important for Cancerians to have a home that is cozy and comfortable, safe and secure. Home is where Cancerians seek peace and refuge.

LEO *July 23–August 23*

THE ZODIAC'S FIFTH SIGN is Leo. The lion, often known as the "King of the Beasts," is the symbol for this sign. Leos share some of the characteristics associated with the lion, being proud, loyal, and fierce. As a fixed sign, Leos are steady characters, and as a fire sign, Leos are attracted to dramatic or creative situations.

LEO GLYPH
The glyph for Leo resembles both the lion's curled tail and the mane of the male lion.

THE LION
The symbol for Leo is the lion. Just as the splendid male lion dominates the family group, Leos, too, like to be at the heart of their families. Leos also enjoy being the center of attention.

Leos are powerful individuals, like lions themselves

ODIAC HOUSES
eo is linked with the
fth house of the
rth chart. This is
e house of
ildren, creativity,
d romance.

FIXED

FIRE

MASCULINE

ZODIAC WHEEL

BODY PART

Leo is traditionally associated
with the heart. Leos are
considered warmhearted and
are happiest when they are
with people they love.

COLOR

The color of gold is
usually associated with
Leo. The metal gold is
linked with Leo, too.

RULERSHIP BOX

★ The ruler of Leo is
the Sun. The glyph
that represents the Sun
is reproduced below.

LEO
JULY 23 – AUGUST 23

Leo

Powerful and proud, Leos like to be at the center of the action. Someone with the Sun or other planets in Leo tends to take responsibility for others and take charge of projects. Leos are dramatic personalities who are warm-hearted and dominant.

Leos can be magnanimous leaders

KINGSHIP
Leo has kingly qualities of pride and leadership. Leos are happiest when they can rule others and be proud of their own acheivements.

FATHER OF THE FAMILY
Leo is the sign of the father. Leos have a strong desire to be the head of a family or to be at the center of a group. Leos take responsibility for those they love and are extremely loyal.

MAKING A MARK

Creativity is associated with planets in Leo.
Painting, drawing, and display are ways of expressing
Leo's creative side. Leos are also connected with
theater and showmanship. They have a very strong
urge to create and to make an impact.

COLORFUL CHARACTERS

Brightly colored flowers such as the
marigold or sunflower are associated with Leo,
as is anything that is sunny, bright,
and colorful. Leos have a sunny disposition
and like to be appreciated.
They are idealists at heart.

VIRGO *August 24–September 22*

THE SIXTH SIGN in the zodiac is Virgo, symbolized by a maiden who carries a stalk of corn. The maiden implies that Virgos are self-contained. Virgo is an earth sign, which signifies practicality. It is also a mutable (or adaptable) sign.

VIRGO GLYPH
The glyph of Virgo represents the maiden with her sheaf of corn.

The corn maiden symbolizes creativity

THE MAIDEN
Traditionally, Virgo's symbol is a corn maiden. The maiden is also linked with the fertile Earth Mother or Moon goddess of ancient myth. The maiden represents a self-sufficient individual. Virgo people have a natural modesty and independence. They need to spend time on their own.

Domestic pets, especially cats and dogs, are associated with Virgo

ZODIAC HOUSES
Virgo is associated with the Sixth house of the birth chart. This house is connected with daily work, health, and diet.

MUTABLE

EARTH

FEMININE

ZODIAC WHEEL

RULERSHIP BOX
★ The planet Mercury is the ruler of Virgo. The glyph below represents Mercury.

BODY PART
Virgo is linked with the intestines. The body's absorption process is associated with Virgo's ability to sift through details.

COLOR
Green is associated with Virgo. Dark brown is also sometimes linked with this sign.

Virgo

Quietly efficient Virgo is known for its
ability to be helpful in many situations.
Virgos are orderly individuals who are
careful in what they say and do. Virgo is
a very analytical and discriminating sign.
Virgos strive for perfection but may be
critical of others. They often feel the
need to straighten up the mess left by
others. Virgos may lack
confidence and
under-value their
own achievements.

VIRGO
AUGUST 24 – SEPTEMBER 22

*Virgo knows
that the mind
and body must
work together*

EXERCISE
People with planets in Virgo in
the birth chart like to keep fit.
Physical as well as mental exercise is
part of their daily life. They prefer a
healthy diet and a healthy way of life.

HEALTHY LIVING
Virgos may suffer from nervous
complaints, such as indigestion
or insomnia. Learning to relax is
essential to a Virgo's health.

*Virgos are
health conscious*

CRAFTSMANSHIP

Virgo is the sign of the craftsman. There is nothing more satisfying to someone with planets in this sign than having the time to do a job well. Tasks requiring careful, detailed work appeal to the perfectionist side of this sign. Virgo concentrates on fine craftsmanship and can sometimes be so focussed on details that he or she loses sight of the bigger picture.

Virgo has an eye for detail

A secure job is important for Virgos

CARING PROFESSIONS

Nursing is a traditional occupation for Virgos. Serving others comes naturally to people with planets in Virgo in their birth chart. Caring for others, attention to detail, and reliability are all Virgo traits.

Virgoans love to be well organized

LIBRA *September 23–October 23*

LIBRA IS THE SEVENTH SIGN of the zodiac. People with Libra prominent in their birth chart have a strong sense of justice. The sign is represented by a pair of scales. As a cardinal sign, Libra implies action. As an air sign, it indicates compromise.

LIBRA GLYPH
Libra's glyph looks something like a pair of scales. It also resembles a bridge.

THE SCALES
Like the scales that represent Libra, Librans seek balance. They are particularly good at evaluating the needs of others. Librans are concerned with harmony and reason. They like to see justice done.

LIBRA – THE SCALES

ZODIAC HOUSES
Libra is linked with the Seventh house of the birth chart, the house of partners and relationships.

ZODIAC WHEEL

CARDINAL

AIR

MASCULINE

RULERSHIP BOX

★ Libra is ruled by the planet Venus. Venus is represented by the glyph below.

♀

BODY PART
Libra rules the kidneys. The kidneys filter the body's waste matter to balance body fluids. Similarly, Librans seek balance in their own lives.

COLOR
All shades of blue, and also blue flowers, such as bluebells and hydrangeas, are linked with Libra.

LIBRA
SEPTEMBER 23 – OCTOBER 23

Libra

Libra is the sign of partnership. People with the Sun or other planets in Libra are natural diplomats and peacemakers. They seek to reconcile differences and prefer to negotiate for peace rather than fight for it. Librans are gifted conversationalists and enjoy active debate. They are able to see all sides of a problem, which can sometimes lead to indecisiveness.

PARTNERSHIPS
For Librans partnerships are paramount. They prefer to be part of a couple and usually work hard to keep their partnership on an even keel. They are sensitive to disharmony and avoid confrontation whenever possible.

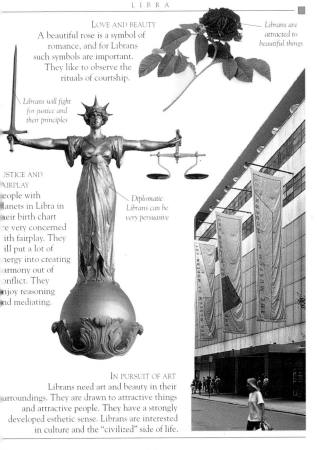

LOVE AND BEAUTY
A beautiful rose is a symbol of
romance, and for Librans
such symbols are important.
They like to observe the
rituals of courtship.

*Librans are
attracted to
beautiful things*

*Librans will fight
for justice and
their principles*

JSTICE AND
AIRPLAY
eople with
lanets in Libra in
eir birth chart
re very concerned
ith fairplay. They
ill put a lot of
nergy into creating
armony out of
onflict. They
njoy reasoning
nd mediating.

*Diplomatic
Librans can be
very persuasive*

THE MUSEUM OF MODERN ART

IN PURSUIT OF ART
Librans need art and beauty in their
urroundings. They are drawn to attractive things
and attractive people. They have a strongly
developed esthetic sense. Librans are interested
in culture and the "civilized" side of life.

SCORPIO October 24–November 22

THE EIGHTH SIGN of the zodiac is Scorpio. Its symbol is the scorpion. Like scorpions, this sign is said to be dangerous when attacked. As a water sign, Scorpio feels emotions intensely.

SCORPIO GLYPH
The glyph that represents Scorpio shows the sting in the tail of the scorpion.

Scorpions sting themselves to death when cornered. Scorpios, too, can be self-destructive

THE SCORPION
Scorpio is represented by the scorpion. This creature gives a painful sting if it is threatened. It also spends most of its life hidden away. Likewise, Scorpio people tend to be forceful and secretive

ZODIAC HOUSES
Scorpio is connected to the eighth house of the birth chart. This is the house of birth, death, and regeneration.

FIXED

WATER

FEMININE

ZODIAC WHEEL

BODY PART
Since ancient times, Scorpio has been linked with the sexual organs. Scorpios' health can suffer as a result of over-indulgence. They are not known for moderation.

RULERSHIP BOX

★ Two planets rule Scorpio. The modern ruler is Pluto and the traditional ruler is Mars.

COLOR
Scorpio is associated with dark colors, especially maroon. Dark red flowers are linked with Scorpio.

Scorpio

As the sign of birth, death, and regeneration, Scorpio is a powerful force in the birth chart. People with planets in Scorpio have a great deal of energy. They are attracted to situations that sometimes seem dangerous to other people. They are fascinated by mystery and eager to penetrate the secrets of the unknown.

SCORPIO
OCTOBER 24 – NOVEMBER 22

Scorpio indicates where great changes will occur

HIDDEN TREASURE
Scorpio is a sign that has hidden depths. People with planets in this sign keep emotions well hidden, and appear brooding and secretive. It may be difficult to penetrate the cool exterior of a Scorpio and find the hidden gems of compassion and fidelity.

CHEMICAL CHANGES
During some chemical reactions the original components undergo a complete change. Scorpio is the sign of change, and in the birth chart it indicates where powerful transformations take place.

THE DARK SIDE OF LIFE

This is a painting by Dante Gabriel Rossetti called *Persephone*. She was goddess of the Underworld, where she lived with Pluto for part of the year. Scorpio, likewise, has links with the darker side of life.

When Persephone was able to visit the world above ground she brought new life with her. She represents springtime after dark winter; Scorpio also signifies renewal.

New shoots indicate regeneration

NEW LIFE

After something as devastating as a volcanic eruption, it is hard to believe that life will return to the landscape. However, new shoots soon begin to grow in the blackened soil. Planets in Scorpio reflect the experience of new life emerging out of destruction.

SAGITTARIUS *November 23–December 21*

SAGITTARIUS IS THE NINTH SIGN of the zodiac. It is symbolized by a centaur, a mythical creature, half man, half horse, and famed as a wild hunter. This sign is associated with seeking knowledge and new challenges, and with a love of travel. Sagittarius is an enthusiastic fire sign and also a restless mutable sign.

SAGITTARIUS GLYPH
The glyph of Sagittarius resembles an arrow shooting skyward.

THE CENTAUR
The symbol for Sagittarius is the centaur. This mythical beast had a horse's body and a man's head and torso, and is usually depicted holding a bow and arrow.

Centaurs had a reputation for riotous living

ZODIAC HOUSES

Sagittarius is the Ninth house of the birth chart. This is the house of the seeker and indicates a desire for knowledge.

ZODIAC WHEEL

MUTABLE

FIRE

MASCULINE

BODY PART

Traditionally, Sagittarius is linked to the thighs. Sagittarians have a tendency to be restless and to enjoy traveling.

COLOR

A rich, dark shade of purple is usually associated with Sagittarius.

RULERSHIP BOX

✶ The planet Jupiter is said to rule the sign of Sagittarius. The glyph below represents the planet Jupiter.

SAGITTARIUS
NOVEMBER 23 – DECEMBER 21

Sagittarius

Sagittarius is the sign of the philosopher.
People with planets in Sagittarius are
seekers and explorers. They are fond of
travel and study. Known to be generous
and expansive, big ideas and grand
visions fill them with enthusiasm.
However, in their excitement
they can be overpowering
and careless about detail.

HIGHER EDUCATION
Sagittarius is connected
with a love of learning.
It is traditionally
associated with higher
education, such as
university or post-
graduate study.

A LOVE OF TRAVEL
People with Sagittarius prominent in their
birth chart love traveling to faraway places.
They enjoy the journey as much as the
destination, and they constantly strive
to extend their horizons.

*Sagittarians
hate to be tied
down*

G-PITZ

QUEST FOR KNOWLEDGE
Optimistic and enthusiastic, Sagittarians
want to understand as much as they can
about the world. They have a restless nature
that looks for spiritual growth.
Sagittarians are seekers who
wish one day to be wise.
They make stimulating
teachers themselves.

*Sagittarians are
honest and
straightforward*

*Sports are a
good outlet for
Sagittarians'
energy*

STRAIGHT TO THE POINT
The typical Sagittarian is very direct, both
in speech and action. Sagittarians can be
restless – they seek out new challenges
and tend to aim high.

PATTERN
Sagittarians
seek patterns
in order to make
sense of life. They
undertake a quest to
find faith and meaning.
They are naturally optimistic,
progressive, and open-minded.

CAPRICORN *December 22–January 20*

THE TENTH SIGN of the zodiac is Capricorn. It is symbolized by a goat, which is sometimes depicted with the tail of a fish. Capricornians develop self-discipline and become sure-footed like a mountain goat. Capricorn is a cardinal, and therefore initiating, sign. It is an Earth sign, and therefore practical.

CAPRICORN GLYPH
This sign's glyph suggests either a bended knee or the curled horn of a goat.

THE GOAT
The symbol for Capricorn is a goat; sometimes the goat is shown with a fish's tail. This creature has ancient mythological associations. Capricorn is linked with the careful and patient behavior of mountain goats.

Just as goats climb to the high mountain peaks, Capricorns seek to climb high in their lives

ZODIAC HOUSES
In the birth chart, the Tenth House is associated with Capricorn. This is the house linked with careers, goals, and vocation.

ZODIAC WHEEL

CARDINAL

EARTH

FEMININE

BODY PART
Capricorn rules the knees and the skeleton. Capricorns can be unyielding individuals who like structure in their lives.

COLOR
Dark gray, black, and dark brown are the colors usually associated with Capricorn.

RULERSHIP BOX

★ Capricorn's ruler is Saturn. The glyph below represents the planet Saturn.

Capricorn

Capricorn is, in general, a serious sign. People with this sign prominent in their birth chart like to be in control and are willing to accept responsibility. Although Capricorns may sometimes feel that they carry a great burden in the world, they work hard to prove their worth and develop patience and reliability.

CAPRICORN
DECEMBER 22 – JANUARY 20

Capricorn respects authority

SCALING THE HEIGHTS
Like a rock climber, Capricorn is willing to make great efforts to reach his goal. However steep the climb to success may be, this is a sign that is able to win through patience and persistence.

DEALING WITH AUTHORITY
Order and structure are part of the Capricorn world. Where Capricorn is emphasized in the birth chart, there is respect for authority and a desire to follow the rules.

SOLID FOUNDATIONS
Firm foundations are very important for Capricorns. They are willing to work hard and build on their achievements, preferring to base projects on their own experience. They have a reputation for steady work and endurance.

PUTTING UP BARRIERS
People with planets in Capricorn can be shy and reserved. They tend to build walls or defenses around themselves that are difficult to penetrate. They are hard to get close to.

Capricorns are solid and reliable

AQUARIUS *January 21–February 18*

ELEVENTH IN THE ZODIAC WHEEL is the sign of Aquarius. It is represented by the water carrier. Someone with planets in this sign likes to be communicative and independent. As a fixed air sign, Aquarians have resolute ideas.

AQUARIUS GLYPH
The glyph for Aquarius suggests waves. These can be seen as the invisible waves that travel through space.

Aquarius, the water carrier, brings new ideas

THE WATER CARRIER
Aquarius is symbolized by a water carrier. The carrier is depicted holding large jugs from which water spills out. The water suggests a cleansing force that washes away the old and stale. In the same way, Aquarius embodies the idea of new thought that brings enlightenment

The water suggests a flow of new thoughts

ODIAC HOUSES
quarius is linked
th the Eleventh
use of the
rth chart. This
he house of hopes,
shes, and ideals.

FIXED

AIR

ASCULINE

ZODIAC WHEEL

BODY PART
Aquarius rules the ankles,
shins, and the circulation
of the blood. Aquarians
are interested in the
circulation of new ideas.

RULERSHIP BOX

★ Uranus is the
modern ruler of
Aquarius. Saturn is
its traditional ruler.

COLOR
Electric blue is Aquarius's
color. It is also associated
with the gemstones
turquoise and aquamarine.

AQUARIUS
JANUARY 21 – FEBRUARY 18

Aquarians keep in touch with current thinking

Aquarius

People with an emphasis on Aquarius in their birth chart have a contradictory side to their nature. They believe in the ideal of equality, but they have a strong will and an individualistic streak. They are driven to rebuild and reform as well as disrupt, revolutionize, and challenge. It is sometimes considered a perverse and unpredictable sign. Aquarians are helpful, though they may remain detached and unemotional.

NEW TECHNOLOGY

People with planets in Aquarius are often comfortable using modern technology. They enjoy experimenting with the latest communication devices. They are said to be progressive and forward-thinking.

FAMILY OF MAN

At the heart of Aquarius is a humanitarian approach to life. People with this sign prominent in their birth chart are said to shy away from close emotional ties and feel more at home with the idea of the universal Family of Man. They are friendly, though they are independent and need to maintain their own personal space.

FAIR SOCIETY

Aquarius believes in a society where all are equal and each is recognized as a unique individual. Organizations such as the United Nations strive to achieve this goal.

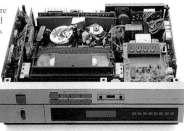

CLEAR THINKING

Aquarians have clear and organized thought processes. They have a scientific approach to life and enjoy finding out how things work.

PISCES *February 19–March 20*

THE TWELFTH AND FINAL SIGN of the zodiac is Pisces. It is represented by two fish swimming in opposite directions. Pisceans are said to be imaginative individuals who, like fish, can appear slippery and indistinct and move with the current. Pisces is a sensitive and compassionate mutable water sign.

PISCES GLYPH
The glyph for Pisces suggests two fishes swimming away from each other.

THE FISHES
Pisces is represented by a symbol showing two fishes pulling in different directions. This apparent conflict reflects the changeable nature of this sign. Pisceans are impressionable and enjoy drifting along like fish in a stream.

The Piscean fish are usually shown linked by a cord

DIAC HOUSES
ces is the Twelfth house
the birth
art, the
use of
vacy,
rets, and
retreat.

MUTABLE

WATER

FEMININE

ZODIAC WHEEL

BODY PART
Pisces, the last sign of the
zodiac, rules the feet. As
well as having sensitive
feet, Pisceans have sensitive,
intuitive natures.

COLOR
Soft sea green is linked
with Pisces. Watery plants
such as water lilies and
willows are also Piscean.

RULERSHIP BOX

★ Neptune is the
modern ruler of Pisces.
The traditional ruler of
Pisces is Jupiter.

Pisces

Pisces is the sign of the romantic and the dreamer. When this sign is prominent in the birth chart, it implies great sensitivity. Pisceans are private people who may feel misunderstood by others. They often enjoy music or art as an outlet for their feelings.

PISCES
FEBRUARY 19 – MARCH 20

Pisceans
feel happ[y]
near wa[ter]

SOOTHING MUSIC
Pisceans usually have intense and private emotions. They find peace as well as enjoyment through listening to or playing music. It may be soothing for their emotions.

CHAMELEONLIKE

Chameleons hide themselves by changing color to blend in with their environment. Pisceans are able to tune into the atmosphere around them and respond accordingly. Their intuition is often very strong.

Pisceans are responsive to the needs of others

LONELY DRIFTER

Pisces can indicate a need to be alone sometimes. This may mean retreating from the world as a way to rest and recuperate. Pisceans may enjoy being on or near water, where they allow themselves to drift along.

GIVING SUPPORT

Pisces is noted for its sympathy and concern for those in trouble. Although they may not respond to demands for sympathy, they will naturally offer support to those in need.

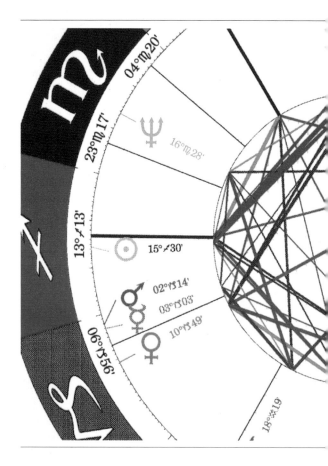

TECHNIQUES

THE BIRTH CHART

The birth chart (sometimes called a horoscope) is a diagram of the heavens. It shows the astrologer the position of the Sun, Moon, and planets for a precise time and place. It is a unique picture of a moment in time.

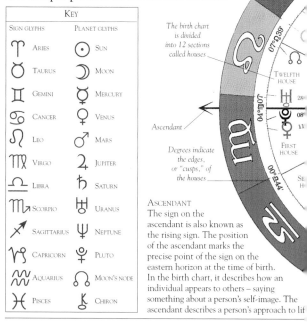

KEY	
SIGN GLYPHS	PLANET GLYPHS
♈ ARIES	☉ SUN
♉ TAURUS	☽ MOON
♊ GEMINI	☿ MERCURY
♋ CANCER	♀ VENUS
♌ LEO	♂ MARS
♍ VIRGO	♃ JUPITER
♎ LIBRA	♄ SATURN
♏ SCORPIO	♅ URANUS
♐ SAGITTARIUS	♆ NEPTUNE
♑ CAPRICORN	♇ PLUTO
♒ AQUARIUS	☊ MOON'S NODE
♓ PISCES	⚷ CHIRON

The birth chart is divided into 12 sections called houses

TWELFTH HOUSE

Ascendant

FIRST HOUSE

Degrees indicate the edges, or "cusps," of the houses

ASCENDANT
The sign on the ascendant is also known as the rising sign. The position of the ascendant marks the precise point of the sign on the eastern horizon at the time of birth. In the birth chart, it describes how an individual appears to others – saying something about a person's self-image. The ascendant describes a person's approach to lif

Midheaven

MIDHEAVEN

The midheaven marks the highest point the Sun reaches in the sky on the day that the chart is set for. In the chart, it stands for what we are known by and how we are recognized. It can indicate what we aspire to in life.

The descendant indicates the degree of the sign setting on the eastern horizon

TENTH HOUSE

NINTH HOUSE

EIGHTH HOUSE

SEVENTH HOUSE

ENTH USE

SIXTH HOUSE

IMUM COELI
The *imum coeli* or IC marks the point of the sky directly opposite the midheaven at the moment of our birth. In the chart, it symbolizes our roots.

The imum coeli

THIRD HOUSE

FIFTH HOUSE

FOURTH HOUSE

There are several house systems. This chart uses the Koch house system

THE HOUSES

The 12 houses describe different areas of daily life. They run counter-clockwise from the ascendant. The planets are distributed through the houses. There are broad links between the characteristics of the First house and those of the first sign, Aries, and between the Second house and Taurus, and so on.

105

Interpreting the chart

When an astrologer has constructed a birth chart, he or she can begin to interpret it. Astrologers look at the positions of the planets in the signs, the position of the ascendant and midheaven. They read the angles and relationships (aspects) between the planets. Finally, they combine all these components to create a picture.

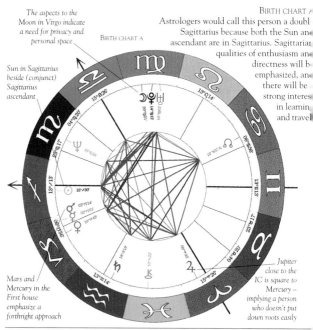

The aspects to the Moon in Virgo indicate a need for privacy and personal space

BIRTH CHART A

Sun in Sagittarius beside (conjunct) Sagittarius ascendant

BIRTH CHART A
Astrologers would call this person a double Sagittarius because both the Sun and ascendant are in Sagittarius. Sagittarian qualities of enthusiasm and directness will be emphasized, and there will be a strong interest in learning and travel.

Mars and Mercury in the First house emphasize a forthright approach

Jupiter close to the IC is square to Mercury – implying a person who doesn't put down roots easily

BIRTH CHART B

The Moon in Aries indicates a warm nature but a tendency to be hasty or impulsive

Virgo ascendant conjunct Pluto and Venus

Jupiter and Chiron oppose the ascendant

Pluto conjunct Venus shows that relationships may be very intense

BIRTH CHART B

In this chart, Pluto and Venus are on the ascendant in Virgo. They are in opposition to Jupiter and Chiron on the descendant. All these planets are square to Mars in the 10th house. This indicates a great deal of energy and tension between the expression of personality and the areas of partnerships and career.

ASPECTS

The glyphs below indicate significant relationships (aspects) between planets.

☌ Conjunction – angle of 0°; combines the planet's energies

✳ Sextile 60°; aspect that indicates co-operation

□ Square 90°; challenging aspect means conflict

△ Trine 120°; the most harmonious aspect

☍ Opposition 180°; aspect that implies tension

PRACTICING ASTROLOGY

FOR MOST PEOPLE, astrology means Sun signs. However, astrology is most useful when an individual birth chart is calculated based on the exact time and place of birth. Astrologers can specialize in different branches of the subject and use charts based on the timing of important events. They can set up charts for companies or countries.

Rodin sculpted The Thinker in 1880

HORARY ASTROLO
This ancient branch
astrology is based on
time the question is
to the astrologer. T
chart is calculated
that moment a
interpreted in order
obtain an answer t
question or determi
the outcome c
course of acti

SELF-KNOWLEDGE
The study of astrology can encourage deeper thought. Natal astrology, which is the study of the birth chart of individuals, can help people understand themselves and the patterns of their life.

WORLD ASTROLOGY
The branch, known as mundane astrology, is concerned with preparing charts of world events and politics. Astrocartographers look at the relationship of an individual's birth chart to those of various countries to determine the best place for him or her to live.

MAP OF THE WORLD

BOARDROOM DECISIONS
Astrologers are sometimes called upon to set up a birth chart for companies and organizations. The chart is based on the time when the company was founded. By studying the charts, astrologers can assess business prospects and suggest favorable times for the company to make key decisions.

FINANCIAL ASTROLOGY
A popular branch of astrology relates the movements of the planets to the rising and falling fortunes of the world's money markets.

QUESTIONS AND ANSWERS

THERE IS A GREAT DEAL of confusion about what astrologers can and cannot do. In particular, astrologers are often asked to predict the future. Questions about the birth charts of twins and Chinese astrology also come up again and again. Some of the most common queries are examined here.

Astrologers use computers to set up the chart

CAN ASTROLOGERS PREDIC
THE FUTUR
Astrologers study regul
cycles of the planets. Base
on past patterns, astrologe
can forecast future possibilitie
Most astrologers do n
believe in a fixed fate, b
believe people can wor
out their own destinie

*A compute
can quickly
calculate a
birth chart*

HOW ARE COMPUTERS USED IN ASTROLOGY?
Computers can be used to calculate the positions of the planets in a birth chart. This laborious work would previously have been done using planetary tables. The art of interpreting the chart, however, is a personal process and requires an experienced astrologer.

WHAT IS CHINESE ASTROLOGY?

Astrology appears in many different cultures. Chinese astrology, like Western astrology, uses 12 different symbols to define 12 basic types. However, Chinese astrology reflects its different culture. It uses the Chinese lunar calendar, the ideas of *yin* (feminine energy) and *yang* (masculine energy), and five elements (wood, fire, earth, metal, and water).

CHINESE
HOROSCOPE WHEEL

WHAT ABOUT TWINS?

Twins born close together in time will have very similar charts. Yet, any variation in time can produce variations in the chart. In this sense every chart is unique. Also, a chart does not describe a fixed destiny, but allows for self-expression.

13

IS THERE A 13TH SIGN?

For nearly 2,000 years astrologers have been using a zodiac based on 12 equal sections of the sky, beginning with Aries at the point of the Spring Equinox. Any new constellation would not form part of this zodiac.

Identical twins may appear similar, but those close to them will notice their differences

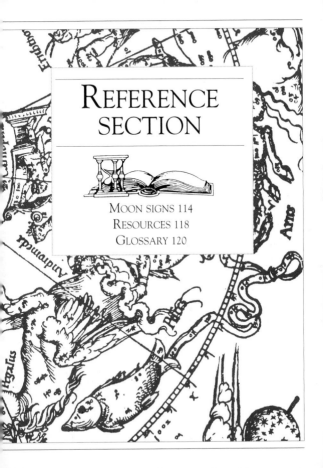

REFERENCE SECTION

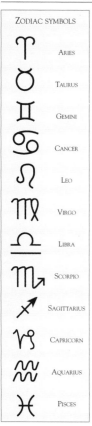

ZODIAC SYMBOLS

♈ ARIES

♉ TAURUS

♊ GEMINI

♋ CANCER

♌ LEO

♍ VIRGO

♎ LIBRA

♏ SCORPIO

♐ SAGITTARIUS

♑ CAPRICORN

♒ AQUARIUS

♓ PISCES

MOON SIGNS

THE MOON MOVES quickly through the zodiac, completing its cycle in 28 days. The Sun and Moon are a complementary pair in the birth chart but, though everyone knows their Sun sign, few people know their Moon sign.

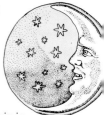

MOON TABLE

To work out your Moon sign look up the year and month of your birth. Note the glyph in that square. Find the date of your birth in the Moon table. Note the number beside your date. Count on that number of glyphs from the glyph you noted earlier. This is your Moon sign.

FOR COMPLETE ACCURACY CHECK YOUR MOON SIGN WITH AN ASTROLOGER.

DAY	ADD	DAY	ADD	DAY	ADD	DAY	ADD
1	0	9	4	17	7	25	11
2	1	10	4	18	7	26	11
3	1	11	5	19	8	27	12
4	1	12	5	20	9	28	12
5	2	13	5	21	9	29	1
6	2	14	6	22	10	30	1
7	3	15	6	23	10	31	2
8	3	16	7	24	10		

Month	1923	1924	1925	1926	1927	1928	1929	1930	1931	1932	1933	1934	1935
January	♊	♏	♈	♌	♐	♈	♍	♑	♉	♎	♓	♋	♏
February	♌	♐	♉	♍	♑	♊	♏	♓	♋	♐	♈	♌	♑
March	♌	♑	♉	♍	♒	♋	♏	♓	♋	♐	♉	♍	♑
April	♎	♓	♋	♏	♈	♍	♑	♉	♍	♒	♊	♎	♓
May	♏	♈	♌	♐	♉	♎	♒	♊	♎	♓	♋	♐	♈
June	♑	♉	♍	♒	♋	♏	♓	♌	♐	♉	♍	♑	♊
July	♒	♋	♏	♓	♌	♐	♈	♍	♑	♊	♎	♓	♋
August	♈	♌	♐	♉	♍	♒	♊	♏	♓	♋	♐	♈	♌
September	♉	♎	♒	♋	♏	♓	♌	♐	♈	♍	♑	♊	♎
October	♊	♏	♓	♌	♐	♉	♍	♑	♉	♎	♓	♋	♏
November	♌	♑	♉	♍	♑	♊	♏	♓	♋	♐	♈	♌	♑
December	♍	♒	♊	♎	♓	♌	♐	♈	♌	♑	♉	♍	♒

Month	1936	1937	1938	1939	1940	1941	1942	1943	1944	1945	1946	1947	1948
January	♈	♌	♑	♉	♍	♒	♊	♎	♓	♌	♐	♈	♍
February	♉	♎	♒	♊	♏	♈	♌	♐	♉	♍	♑	♊	♎
March	♊	♎	♒	♋	♐	♈	♌	♐	♉	♎	♒	♊	♏
April	♌	♐	♈	♌	♑	♉	♎	♒	♋	♏	♌	♎	♑
May	♍	♑	♉	♎	♒	♊	♏	♓	♌	♐	♈	♍	♒
June	♎	♒	♋	♏	♈	♌	♑	♉	♎	♒	♊	♏	♓
July	♏	♈	♌	♑	♉	♍	♒	♊	♏	♓	♌	♐	♈
August	♑	♉	♎	♒	♋	♏	♈	♌	♐	♉	♍	♑	♊
September	♓	♋	♏	♈	♌	♑	♉	♍	♒	♋	♏	♓	♌
October	♈	♌	♑	♉	♎	♒	♊	♎	♓	♌	♐	♈	♍
November	♊	♎	♒	♊	♏	♈	♌	♐	♉	♍	♑	♊	♏
December	♋	♏	♓	♌	♑	♉	♍	♑	♊	♎	♒	♋	♐

Month	1949	1950	1951	1952	1953	1954	1955	1956	1957	1958	1959	1960	196_
January	♑	♊	♎	♓	♋	♏	♈	♌	♑	♉	♍	♒	♋
February	♓	♋	♐	♈	♍	♑	♉	♎	♒	♊	♏	♈	♌
March	♓	♋	♐	♉	♍	♑	♊	♏	♓	♋	♏	♈	♌
April	♉	♍	♒	♊	♎	♓	♋	♐	♈	♌	♑	♊	
May	♊	♎	♓	♋	♐	♈	♍	♑	♉	♎	♒	♋	♏
June	♌	♐	♈	♍	♑	♊	♎	♓	♋	♐	♈	♌	♑
July	♍	♑	♊	♎	♓	♋	♏	♈	♌	♑	♉	♍	♒
August	♏	♓	♋	♐	♈	♍	♑	♉	♎	♒	♊	♏	
September	♐	♈	♍	♑	♊	♎	♒	♋	♐	♈	♌	♑	
October	♑	♊	♎	♓	♋	♏	♓	♌	♑	♉	♍	♒	♋
November	♓	♋	♏	♈	♍	♑	♉	♎	♒	♊	♏	♈	♌
December	♈	♌	♑	♊	♎	♒	♊	♏	♓	♌	♐	♉	♍

Month	1962	1963	1964	1965	1966	1967	1968	1969	1970	1971	1972	1973	197_
January	♏	♓	♌	♐	♈	♍	♑	♊	♎	♒	♋	♐	♈
February	♐	♉	♍	♒	♊	♏	♓	♋	♏	♈	♍	♑	♉
March	♐	♉	♎	♒	♊	♏	♈	♌	♐	♉	♍	♑	♊
April	♒	♋	♏	♈	♌	♑	♉	♍	♒	♊	♏	♓	♋
May	♓	♌	♐	♉	♍	♒	♊	♎	♓	♋	♐	♈	♍
June	♉	♎	♒	♊	♏	♓	♌	♐	♉	♍	♑	♊	♎
July	♊	♏	♓	♌	♐	♈	♍	♑	♊	♎	♓	♋	♐
August	♌	♐	♉	♎	♒	♊	♏	♓	♋	♏	♈	♍	♑
September	♍	♒	♋	♏	♓	♋	♐	♉	♍	♑	♊	♎	♓
October	♏	♓	♌	♐	♈	♍	♒	♊	♎	♒	♋	♐	♈
November	♐	♉	♎	♒	♊	♎	♓	♋	♐	♈	♍	♑	♉
December	♑	♊	♏	♓	♋	♐	♈	♌	♑	♉	♎	♒	♏

Month	1975	1976	1977	1978	1979	1980	1981	1982	1983	1984	1985	1986	1987
JANUARY	♌	♑	♉	♍	♒	♊	♏	♓	♌	♐	♉	♍	♑
FEBRUARY	♎	♒	♋	♏	♈	♌	♐	♉	♍	♒	♊	♎	♓
MARCH	♎	♓	♋	♏	♈	♍	♑	♉	♎	♒	♊	♏	♓
APRIL	♐	♈	♍	♑	♊	♎	♒	♋	♏	♈	♌	♌	♒
MAY	♑	♉	♎	♒	♋	♏	♓	♌	♐	♉	♍	♒	♊
JUNE	♓	♋	♐	♈	♌	♑	♉	♎	♒	♊	♏	♓	♌
JULY	♈	♌	♑	♊	♍	♒	♏	♓	♌	♐	♉	♍	♍
AUGUST	♉	♎	♓	♋	♏	♈	♌	♐	♈	♎	♒	♊	♎
SEPTEMBER	♋	♐	♈	♌	♒	♊	♎	♒	♊	♏	♓	♌	♐
OCTOBER	♌	♑	♉	♍	♒	♋	♏	♓	♋	♐	♉	♍	♑
NOVEMBER	♎	♓	♋	♏	♓	♌	♐	♉	♍	♒	♊	♎	♓
DECEMBER	♏	♈	♌	♒	♉	♍	♑	♊	♎	♋	♐	♐	♈

Month	1988	1989	1990	1991	1992	1993	1994	1995	1996	1997	1998	1999	2000
JANUARY	♊	♎	♒	♋	♏	♈	♌	♑	♉	♎	♒	♋	♏
FEBRUARY	♋	♐	♈	♍	♑	♉	♎	♒	♋	♏	♈	♌	♐
MARCH	♌	♐	♉	♍	♒	♊	♎	♓	♋	♏	♈	♌	♑
APRIL	♍	♒	♊	♏	♓	♋	♐	♈	♍	♉	♊	♎	♓
MAY	♏	♓	♌	♐	♈	♍	♉	♎	♒	♋	♏	♏	♌
JUNE	♐	♉	♍	♑	♊	♎	♓	♋	♐	♈	♌	♑	♉
JULY	♑	♊	♎	♒	♋	♐	♈	♌	♑	♉	♎	♒	♊
AUGUST	♓	♌	♐	♈	♍	♑	♉	♎	♓	♋	♏	♓	♌
SEPTEMBER	♉	♍	♑	♊	♏	♓	♋	♏	♈	♌	♑	♉	♎
OCTOBER	♊	♎	♒	♐	♐	♈	♌	♑	♉	♎	♒	♊	♏
NOVEMBER	♌	♐	♈	♍	♑	♉	♎	♒	♋	♏	♈	♌	♑
DECEMBER	♍	♑	♉	♎	♒	♋	♏	♈	♌	♐	♉	♍	♒

Resources

There are a number of ways to learn more about astrology. You can attend one of the major schools in the larger cities of the world. You can also learn from local education centers. There are correspondence courses run by teaching organizations, some of which offer full diploma courses and qualifications. Some schools and courses are listed below.

ASTROLOGICAL EDUCATION

Aquarian Age Astrologer
124 East 24th Street
New York, NY 10016
212/777-6464

Astro-Psychology Institute
2640 Greenwich, Suite 403
San Francisco, CA 94123
415/921-1192

National Council for
Geocosmic Research, Inc.
P.O. Box 3236
New York, NY 10185
212/255-3236

ASSOCIATIONS

American Federation of
Astrologers
Robert W. Cooper,
Executive Secretary
P.O. Box 22040
Tempe, AZ 85285
602/838-1751

Maintains special library and offers astrological software referral services, conducts astrological examinations of persons, operates speakers' bureau, compiles statistics, publishes periodicals.

Association for
Astrological Psychology
Glenn Perry, Ph.D.,
President
360 Quietwood Drive
San Rafael, CA 94903
415/382-0304
Works to establish general guidelines for the application of astrology in the fields of counseling and psychotherapy. Publishes newsletter.

Astro-Psychology Institute
Milo Kovar, Dir.
2640 Greenwich, Suite 403
San Fransisco, CA 94123
415/921-1192

Conducts seminars and classes, maintains speakers bureau and charitable program, compiles statistics, publishes books.

Astromusic
Gerald Jay Markoe,
Contact
P.O. Box 118
New York, NY 10033
212/942-0004
Translates person's horoscope or birth chart into a musical composition on cassette, intended to enhance meditation, relaxation, and healing.

Friends of Astrology
Gladys Hall, President
535 Woodside Avenue
Hinsdale, IL 60521
708/654-4737
Maintains biographical archives and library, operates speakers' bureau, compiles statistics. Holds

tures, publishes
lletin.

ternational Society for
strological Research
rol Tebbs, Secretary
). Box 38613
s Angeles,
A 90038-0613
8/333-8702
ovides research data and
ucation for professional
rologers.

OOK SOURCES

ewellyn Publications
). Box 64383
Paul, MN 55164-0383

ystical Shop
3 West 82nd Street
ew York, NY 10024
2/799-5686

ew York Astrology Center
0 Lexington Avenue
ew York, NY
2/949-7275

muel Weiser Booksellers
ox 612
rk Beach, ME 03910

ilshire Book Company
015 Sherman Road
orth Hollywood,
A 91605

SOFTWARE SOURCES

American Federation of
Astrologers, Inc.
P.O. Box 22040
Tempe, AZ 85285-2040

Astrolabe
P.O. Box 28
Orleans, MA 02653

Astroresearch
1500 Massachusetts
Avenue, NW
Suite 764
Washington, DC 20005

Matrix Software
315 Marion Avenue
Big Rapids, MI 49307

PERIODICALS

*The American Astrology
Magazine*
475 Park Avenue
New York, NY 10016

Dell Horoscope Magazine
P.O. Box 53352
Boulder, CO 80521-1511

The Ascendent
P.O. Box 10631
Wetherfield, CT 06109

Aspects
P.O. Box 556
Encino, CA 91426

Astro-Analytics
16440 Haynes Street
Van Nuys, CA 91406-5717

Astro-Talk Bulletin
315 Marion Avenue
Grand Rapids, MI 49307

Cosmobiology International
P.O. Box 10631
Denver, CO 80210

Geocosmic News
78 Hubbard Avenue
Stamford, CT 06906

The Horary Practitioner
1420 NW Gillman
Suite 2154
Issaquah, WA 98027-5327

Kosmos
P.O. Box 38613
Los Angeles, CA 90038

Mutable Dilemma
5953 W. 86th Street
Los Angeles, CA 90045

Urania
330 E
New York, NY 10017

Welcome to Planet Earth
The Great Bear
P.O. Box 5164
Eugene, OR 97405

Glossary

AIR
One of the four elements into which the signs are divided. The three air signs are Gemini, Libra, and Aquarius. In astrology, air represents thoughts, ideas, and communication.

ANGLE
There are four angles in the birth chart: ascendant, midheaven, descendant, and *imum coeli*. In most house systems, these mark the cusps of the First, Tenth, Seventh, and Fourth houses, respectively.

ARCHETYPE
Comes from two Greek words *arche* (original) and *typos* (model). It signifies something that is common to everyone. Planets and signs are archetypes of human behavior.

ASCENDANT
The point in the zodiac on the eastern horizon of the birth chart. Also known as the rising sign. It is the cusp of

the First house, which is associated with appearance and personality.

ASPECT
The angle measured in degrees between planets, or significant points in the birth chart.

ASTROLOGY
The study of celestial bodies and their cycles and the correlation between them and events on Earth. The word comes from two Greek words, *astron* (star) and *logos* (knowing). It is the interpretation of the planets and their cycles.

ASTRONOMY
The study, naming, and cataloging of celestial bodies.

BIRTH CHART
A diagram representing the positions of the Sun, Moon, and planets at a particular time and place as seen from Earth. Sometimes known as a horoscope or map.

CARDINAL
One of the three qualities into which the signs are divided. The four cardinal signs are: Aries, Cancer, Libra, and Capricorn. In astrology, cardinal is the active, initiating quality.

CELESTIAL SPHERE
The view of the heavens as seen from Earth – as if the Earth were at the center and the stars lay above it like a dome.

CHINESE ASTROLOGY
A system of astrology based on the lunar calendar. It has 12 creatures representing 12 basic types.

CIRCLE
The glyphs of the planets are made up of the circle, crescent, and cross. The circle represents spirit.

CONJUNCTION
A term describing two or more planets lying next to each other in the birth chart.

CONSTELLATION
A cluster of stars named after the picture they represented to early stargazers.

CRESCENT
One of the three shapes that form the glyphs of the planets. The crescent represents soul.

CROSS
One of the three shapes that form the glyphs of the planets. The cross represents matter.

CUSP
The point that separates the signs or houses in the birth chart.

CYCLE
Astrology studies the cycles or orbits of the planets.

DEGREE
The birth chart is divided into 360 degrees. The parts of the chart are measured in degrees.

DESCENDANT
The point of the zodiac on the western horizon of the birth chart. It is the cusp of the seventh house. The descendant is associated with partnership.

EARTH
One of the four elements into which the signs are divided. The three Earth signs are Taurus, Virgo, and Capricorn. In astrology, Earth represents practicality, reliability, and the material world.

ECLIPTIC
The Sun's apparent path through the heavens, seen from the Earth, as it moves through the year.

ELEMENT
The 12 signs are divided into four elements: fire, earth, air, and water. They can be loosely linked with the medieval idea of humors: choleric (fiery), melancholic (earthy), sanguine (airy), and phlegmatic (watery).

EPHEMERIS
Tables listing daily planetary positions and other imformation necessary for drawing up the birth chart. This information is now available on various computer software.

FEMININE SIGNS
The 12 zodiac signs are divided into six feminine and six masculine signs, also known as negative and positive. The feminine signs are traditionally associated with receptivity. The six feminine signs are: Taurus, Virgo, Capricorn, Cancer, Scorpio, and Pisces.

FIRE
One of the four elements into which the signs are divided. The three fire signs are Aries, Leo, and Sagittarius. Fire represents vitality, enthusiasm, and spirit.

FIXED
One of the three qualities into which the signs are divided. The four fixed signs are Taurus, Leo, Scorpio, and Aquarius. In astrology, fixed is a stable and steady quality.

FORECAST
Astrological assessment of future trends based on planetary patterns.

GLYPH

A character or symbol that stands for an object or idea. The planets and signs have glyphs that are recognized by astrologers in the Western world.

GMT

This stands for Greenwich Mean Time. It divides the world into time zones beginning at 0° in Greenwich, London, UK. In drawing a birth chart, local time is converted to GMT.

HORARY ASTROLOGY

The art of judging a horoscope that was set up for the time the astrologer was asked a specific question.

HOROSCOPE

A diagram that shows the positions of the planets at a particular time and place. It is also known as a birth chart.

HOUSES

The 12 divisions of the birth chart. The chart represents the heavens divided into four. Each quarter is divided into three, giving 12 houses.

HOUSE SYSTEMS

There are different systems to divide the birth chart into houses. These house systems include: Koch, Equal, and Placidus.

IMUM COELI

Often abbreviated to IC. It indicates the point of the chart opposite the midheaven. From a Latin term meaning "lowest part of heaven." In most house systems it is the cusp of the Fourth house.

MASCULINE SIGN

The 12 signs are divided into six masculine signs and six feminine signs, also called positive and negative. The masculine signs are traditionally associated with an outgoing disposition. The six masculine signs are: Aries, Gemini, Leo, Libra, Sagittarius, and Aquarius.

MIDHEAVEN

The midheaven marks the highest point the Sun reaches during the day of the birth chart.

MOON'S NODE

The point where the Moon's orbit crosses the ecliptic. The North node is also called Dragon's Head, and the South, Dragon's Tail.

MUNDANE ASTROLOGY

From the Latin word mundus meaning the world. "Mundane" astrology studies planetary cycles that affect nations, countries, and politics.

MUTABLE

One of the three qualities into which the signs are divided. The four mutable signs are Gemini, Virgo, Sagittarius, and Pisces. In astrology, mutable refers to the quality of adaptability and changeability.

NATAL ASTROLOGY

The interpretation of an individual's birth chart.

OPPOSITION

An angle of 180° between planets in the birth chart, which implies tension between the planets involved.

ORRERY
A clockwork model of the solar system showing the Sun orbited by the planets. It is named after the Earl of Orrery who had a model built in 1712.

PLANET
There are nine planets in the solar system, including the Earth. In astrology, the term planet is used to include the Sun and the Moon.

QUALITY
The 12 signs are divided into three qualities: cardinal, fixed, and mutable.

RISING SIGN
Also called the ascendant. The sign on the eastern horizon at the moment of birth shown on the birth chart.

RULERSHIP
A traditional expression for the link between a planet with a sign. For example, Mars rules Aries; it also rules emotions such as anger, qualites such as heat, and objects such as iron.

SEXTILE
An angle of 60° between planets in the birth chart. It implies cooperation between the planets involved.

SIGNS
The 12 signs of the zodiac are the 12 equal 30° divisions of the ecliptic around the Earth. The first sign is Aries and the last sign is Pisces.

SQUARE
An angle of 90° between planets in the birth chart, which implies friction between the planets involved.

SUN SIGN
The sign through which the Sun is passing at the time of birth. People often refer to their Sun sign as their "Star sign." Sun sign horoscopes are published in many magazines and newspapers. For most astrologers, the Sun sign is important but it is only one of a number of important factors in the birth chart.

TRINE
An angle of 120° between planets in the birth chart. This relationship indicates harmony between the planets involved.

SYMBOLIC
Using one thing to describe another. It is a way to express abstract concepts.

WATER
One of the four elements into which the signs are divided. The water signs are Cancer, Scorpio, and Pisces. Water represents feeling, emotions, and soul in astrology.

ZODIAC
The complete set of 12 signs that forms a circle called, in Greek, the "Circle of Life." There are two zodiacs: Sidereal and Tropical. Western astrologers use the Tropical, which begins at the point f the Spring Equinox. Indian astrology uses the Sidereal, which keeps its ancient connection with the constellations.

Index

Acknowledgements

Dorling Kindersley would like to thank: Hilary Bird for the index, Caroline Potts for photo research, Anna Kruger for additional astrological information, Louise Cox for design assistance, and Robert Currey at The Astrology Shop, 78 Neal Street, London for providing the birth charts.

Photographs by:
Peter Anderson, Paul Bricknell, Geoff Brightling, Peter Chadwick, Andy Crawford, Geoff Dann, Steve Gorton, Frank Greenaway, Stephen Hayward, John Heseltine, Jacqui Hurst, Colin Keates, Keith Kent, Dave King, Monique Le Luhandre, Norman McGrath, Ray Mollier, David Murray, Stephen Oliver, Susanna Price, Tim Ridley, Kim Sayer, Jules Selme, Karl Shone, Stephen Shot, Clive Streeter, James Stevenson, Jane Stockman, Matthew Ward, Rodney Wilson.

Illustrations by:
Luciano Corbella, Brian Delf, Bob Garwood, Taurus Graphics, Peter Griffiths, Barry Jones, Danuta Mayer, Guy Smith.

Modelmaking by Peter Griffiths.

The Publisher would like to thank the following for their kind permission to reproduce the photographs:

t=top c=center a=above b=below l=left r=right.

Bridgeman Art Library: Galleria degli Uffizi, Florence front cover br, 35l, Tate Gallery, London 83tr, Musee Rodin, Paris, 108bl; Corbis / Bettmann / UPI: 43cl; Stephen Costello: 110cl; ET Archive: 38bl; Mary Evans Picture Library: 10-11, 16bl, 17tc, 26cb, 40bl, 46bl, Explorer 28r; The Falco Family: 95t; GeoScience Features Picture Library: Dr B Booth 83cl; Bev Goodwin 80bl; Mike Hoborn: 69cl; The Image Bank: Brett Froomer 109b, John P Kelly 100-101b; LAT Photographic: 56b; NASA: 12tr, 24-25, 29br 31br; Oddball International, London: 65r; Rex Features Ltd: 47l; Science Museum: 95br; Science Photo Library: Keith Kent 43c; Tony Stone Images: Kevin Nichol 77tr; Rodney Wilson: 30-31b.

Every effort has been made to trace the copyright holders. Dorling Kindersley apologise for any unintentional omissions and would be pleased to insert the appropriate acknowledgement in any future editions of this book.